365+ WAYS

COUPLES GROW APART
WITHOUT REALIZING IT
AND HOW TO RECLAIM
YOUR CLOSENESS

THIS BOOK IS GIVEN TO:

recipient

because I care about our/your relationship.

NAME   DATE

PUBLISHED BY
Positive Psyche. Biz
P. O. Box 142
Lothian, MD
United States of America

Lost Love
ISBN 978-0-9827636-1-2
www.loveislost.com
LIBRARY OF CONGRESS PCN: 2010915233

More Books and Products by Enrique Ruiz:

Lost Love: The Game©
The Ultimate Relationship-Building Game for Couples
ISBN 978-0-9827636-2-9
www.loveislost.com/game

Wisher, Washer, Wishy-Washy
Hardcover: ISBN 978-0-615-37111-5
Paperback: ISBN 978-0-615-25240-7
www.wisherwasher.com

Discriminate or Diversify
Hardcover: ISBN 978-0-615-25760-0
Paperback: ISBN 978-0-578-01734-1
www.humandiversity.biz

The "W" Characters
ISBN 978-0-9827636-0-5
www.characterforchildren.com

www.positivepsyche.biz
A **PositivePsyche.Biz** book
www.americasdiversityleader.com

LOST LOVE

365+ WAYS
COUPLES GROW APART
WITHOUT REALIZING IT
AND HOW TO RECLAIM
YOUR CLOSENESS

—ENRIQUE & SARAH RUIZ—

A PositivePsyche.biz Book
Maryland, U.S.A.

CONTENTS

A THANK YOU

We would like to thank Taylor Mallory for her superb editing, personal engagement and additions to this publication, and Jennifer Tyson for the outstanding support with graphic layout.

We would like to thank the many friends who added their own insightful pearls of wisdom; and Melinda Emert.

We are most grateful to each other and for a second chance at love, one that mesmerizes us and enchants our worlds. We are both fortunate to be wiser the second time around.

INTRODUCTION

Most people would agree that "love" is a hard word to define, if only because everyone defines it differently. Poets have been putting the feeling into words for as long as there has been written language, and while some have done better jobs of it than others, the fact remains: Love is intangible and subjective to the experiences and temperament of each lover.

The dictionary defines love as follows:

1) A deep, tender, ineffable feeling of affection and solicitude toward a person, such as that arising from kinship, recognition of attractive qualities, or a sense of underlying oneness.

2) A feeling of intense desire and attraction toward a person with whom one is disposed to make a pair; the emotion of sex and romance.

3) Sexual passion. Sexual intercourse. A love affair.

4) A person who is the object of deep or intense affection or attraction; beloved. Often used as a term of endearment. The mutual affection and ardor of lovers: passion, amorousness, amour, love, fervor, fire, rapture, ecstasy, intoxication, heart.

Society, on the other hand, defines love with kisses, candles, roses and rings – and, in part, with fairy tales. And the beginning stages of a long romance *can* feel like a fairy tale. It all starts with Cupid's arrow. In the excitement and passion of a new romance, couples feel that they are on the road to happiness and emotional bliss.

First comes love … and then, for many, comes marriage. For several thousand years and in many cultures, men and women have exchanged rings (or other symbolic items), performed certain rituals and taken wedding vows, solemn promises to live and act in a caring, loving fashion with their soul mates – and to never part. Good intentions abound!

Over time, however, disappointment invariably settles into many unions. Disagreements, misunderstandings, busy schedules and lost opportunities get in the way. We think that our partners should automatically understand what we need, but they often don't; we just "know" that partners automatically feel our feelings (our triumphs and hurts), but they don't; we trust that our words convey our fears and insecurities, but they don't.

When the road gets rocky, we often hearken back to our early days (when Cupid was still frolicking in our midst) and feel that by silently yelling, *"You're wrong, so fix it!"* to our spouses, we will solve our marital difficulties. Unfortunately, these cries all too often crescendo into yelling matches (or silent "cold wars") that do not get resolved. We unconsciously mute the "hear me" cries of our loved ones, for we, too, are busy crying, "Hear me." Tempo and volume increase as each partner tries to get his or her point across, but our dialogues can become like two ships passing in the night, completely unaware of each other's presence.

We know this not because we are trained psychologists or relationship "experts," but because we have lived it.

I (Enrique) was married for 25 years to a very pretty woman with whom I shared a religious upbringing (we were both pastor's kids) and a desire to build a family and a life. In our early dating days, we became infatuated with one another in a way that only young people can. We hadn't experienced enough of love to know what could come. We'd both seen plenty of movies and read plenty of books with descriptions of love. But we had no manual to warn us about what happens after the cameras stop rolling – after "happily ever after." We had no idea about the slippery slope we would *slowly* and inadvertently create for ourselves. Now that I know what can go wrong, I know which landmines to avoid the second time around, as I complete my life's journey with my new wife and soul-mate, Sarah.

I (Sarah) married young, full of idealistic expectations that neither of us could live up to. I wanted the fairy-tale wedding and the "happily ever after" without having any idea how to incorporate personal struggles, or even growth, into it. My first husband and I made many of the most common marriage mistakes, but what doomed us beyond repair was that we never learned how to communicate with each other. Not only did we fail to meet one another's expectations, but we also failed to express the disappointment until it was too late. Writing this book gave me an opportunity to gain clarity around how I communicate my expectations so that I can relate better as a wife and partner to Enrique. I hope that this book gives you some insight and even some "aha" moments so that you can make a difference in your relationship.

Marriages don't just fall apart one day. There are always lots of signs – pretty common-sense stuff that, when we neglect to consider in relationships, invariably degenerate our bonds. But common sense is, unfortunately, not always common – especially when emotions run high. Selfish motives, misunderstandings, preconceived notions, unrealistic expectations and busy lives all interfere with our ability to see our relationships (and ourselves) clearly. Divorce is a painful process for everyone. Children are confused, people take sides, and a sense of loss permeates the air.

The purpose of this book is to help you identify and focus on the things – big and small – that can slowly tear love apart, so you'll know the warning signs to look for and to avoid, and how to reignite love once it has been damaged.

In Section I, "Love Is Weakened When," we'll list some of those warning signs – both the big red flags and the seemingly innocuous "little" things – that indicate something is wrong, and we'll discuss which pitfalls to avoid. Some of these we have drawn from our own relationships, and some come from friends, co-workers and family members whose relationships have also slowly deteriorated. Section I is a *"what not to do"* guide to relationships, designed to help you become more aware of ways romantic partners hurt and push one another away (often without meaning to or even knowing they're doing it).

If you recognize your relationship in Section I, that doesn't mean your love is doomed. It just means your romance needs some maintenance, and being aware of the problem is, after all, the first step to changing things.

Want a more understanding, satisfying relationship with your partner? Section II, "Love Is Felt When," provides the flip side of the "Love Is Weakened When" sentiments from the first section. Here, we'll list ways that we show or feel love – ways that we make our partners feel like the most important people in the world.

And in Section III, "Love Is Reignited When," we'll suggest ways to reconnect with your partner, strengthen your bond and restore harmony in your home.

In our humble opinions, one of the best and most eloquent definitions of love appears in the Bible. Regardless of your faith (for this verse is not about Christianity), consider the implications of this quotation:

Love is very patient and kind, never jealous or envious,
never boastful or proud, never haughty or selfish or rude. Love does
not demand its own way. It is not irritable or touchy. It does not hold grudges
and will hardly even notice when others do it wrong. It is never glad about injustice,
but rejoices whenever truth wins out. If you love someone you will be loyal to
him no matter what the cost. You will always believe in him, always expect
the best of him, and always stand your ground in defending him.

1 CORINTHIANS 13: 4-7

We like this description of love because it takes into account that we are not perfect people and that we do not lead blissfully perfect, fairy-tale lives. Relationships made up of two imperfect people require patience, kindness, forgiveness and trust. We believe the secret of lasting love is to:

L isten
O verlook Faults
V oice Approval
E ncourage Each Other

In our previous marriages, we learned from the challenges and pain. Now we are moving on, knowing what not to do the second time around. And we want to share it with you. It can be really hard to see the light when we're in the middle of the storm, to see what's right in front of us when we're mired in insecurity, loneliness and misery.

We trust that you can learn from our observations and experiences so that you can reignite your *lost love* with a very special person – whether it's with your current partner or with someone new. We have. We are madly in love with each other and are both thrilled to be in a relationship with someone who makes us feel like we have always wanted to feel and with whom we have similar values on everything we consider important in romantic partnerships – children, family, aspirations for the future, investing time in each other, money, physical closeness, exercise, and a shared sensibility for music, movies and books. After the pain of the

storms we have weathered, we have truly found our place in the sun – together.
And we wish you, and yours, every success!

Sign up for our periodic newsletter at
www.loveislost.com
for more tips on how to enhance your relationships.

*"Love is blind, and lovers cannot see
the petty follies that themselves commit."*

WILLIAM SHAKESPEARE

*"Love never dies of starvation,
but often of indigestion."*

FRENCH PROVERB

—SECTION 1—

LOVE IS WEAKENED WHEN...

When we enter marriages or other serious long-term relationships, most of us do so expecting (or at least hoping) that they will work out, that we have found the soul mates with whom we'll spend the rest of our lives. However, many of these relationships end in disappointment and heartbreak.

Why? Why do we fail to connect? Why do we fail to properly communicate our feelings and expectations? And what's more, why do we often fail to notice the warning signs until it's too late?

It's easy to take our relationships for granted, to not notice the things we're doing (or not doing) that are slowly deteriorating the relationships that we treasure. Over time, we can lose perspective and settle into patterns that aren't making us happy but that have become such status quo that we accept them.

The passages in this section take many of the very real and complex issues that plague relationships and condense them down into a simple checklist of what not to do – both the major red flags and the seemingly harmless actions that can build up over time into a big deal. Chances are, you're guilty of at least a few of these (we all are), and being aware of that will help you address those behaviors. If you identify with too many of these for your own comfort, you'll know that your relationship isn't working, at least not on its current trajectory. Either way, knowing what not to do is at least half the battle.

1 Love is **weakened** when…
You marry to live happily ever after but live haplessly ever after.

2 Love is **weakened** when…
You hunger for laughter and feed one another with insults.

3 Love is **weakened** when…
You withhold everything – or you withhold nothing.

4 Love is **weakened** when…
You view apologizing as a sign of weakness.

5 Love is **weakened** when…
You don't care what your spouse does for a living.

6 Love is **weakened** when...
You kick your partner when he is down to make yourself feel strong.

7 Love is **weakened** when...
You are treated as an inconvenience – or as a mere convenience.

8 Love is **weakened** when...
You give feedback; he hears criticism.

9 Love is **weakened** when...
She puts you down in front of others.

TO LOVE, AND BE LOVED ... BEGINS WITH ME.

How do these statements apply to me?
What can I DO to make our love grow?
USE THIS SPACE TO ANNOTATE YOUR THOUGHTS

" ... A simple 'I love you' means more than money ... "

FRANK SINATRA

10 Love is **weakened** when...
Your measure your importance by how much sympathy you can sap.

11 Love is **weakened** when...
Your receptionist screens your spouse's calls to keep
your adrenaline level low.

12 Love is **weakened** when...
Today is not good enough, the past is where you want to be,
and the future is more of today.

13 Love is **weakened** when...
You would rather cry than try.

14 Love is **weakened** when...
You avoid playing board games together because you can't even
"play house" without an argument.

15 Love is **weakened** when...
Your partner angers readily when others praise you.

16 Love is **weakened** when...
Negative input from friends and family become self-fulfilling
prophecies in your relationship.

17 Love is **weakened** when...
Your vices cause trouble on the home front.

18 Love is **weakened** when...
You feel that your life together is a facade – lovely on the outside,
pathetic on the inside.

19 Love is **weakened** when…
You allow simmering guilt to destroy the union you have built.

20 Love is **weakened** when…
You no longer do things for one another because you want to,
but rather because you "have to."

21 Love is **weakened** when…
Your spouse never asks about your day and only shares about
his on a "need-to-know" basis.

22 Love is **weakened** when…
Fear of change keeps you in the same rut.

23 Love is **weakened** when…
Separate vacations 3,000 miles apart barely give you
enough space from each other.

24 Love is **weakened** when…
Your spouse treats you as a subordinate to your children's desires.

AGELESS RELATIONSHIP WISDOM

"The wise man does not lay up treasure.
The more he gives, the more he has."
CHINESE PROVERB

"He gives double who gives unasked."
ARABIAN PROVERB

25 Love is **weakened** when...
You persistently justify injustices committed.

26 Love is **weakened** when...
You stop *liking* each other.

27 Love is **weakened** when...
You need a buzz to enjoy (or tolerate) time alone with your spouse.

28 Love is **weakened** when...
Personal insecurity weakens your relationship bonds.

29 Love is **weakened** when...
You avoid your friends and family because you're afraid they'll tell you the truth.

30 Love is **weakened** when...
You vilify your spouse in front of your children.

31 Love is **weakened** when...
Affection is treated like an infection.

32 Love is **weakened** when...
The holidays approach, and 'tis the "season to be mad."

33 Love is **weakened** when...
Your opinions don't matter to each other.

34 Love is **weakened** when...
Business trips provide a welcome separation.

35 Love is **weakened** when...
Your spouse only takes your calls in the case of dire emergency.

36 Love is **weakened** when…
You don't live by the standards you set for your partner.

37 Love is **weakened** when…
You can't get the caresses you long for.

38 Love is **weakened** when…
Your wife suddenly wants to discard your surname and
re-adopt her maiden name.

39 Love is **weakened** when…
What once made you laugh now makes you cringe.

40 Love is **weakened** when…
You hear, "I am only with you because of my relationship with God."

41 Love is **weakened** when…
Your spouse can hang up on you without batting an eye.

42 Love is **weakened** when…
You only stay, because the children need you.

AGELESS RELATIONSHIP WISDOM

*"The shoe that fits one person pinches another;
there is no recipe for living that suits all cases."*
CARL JUNG

"The course of true love never did run smooth."
WILLIAM SHAKESPEARE

43 Love is **weakened** when...
Your spouse tramples your feelings as if they were unwanted weeds.

44 Love is **weakened** when...
Ill will becomes a contagious disease.

45 Love is **weakened** when...
You rarely talk to one another for fear of being hit by spoken arrows.

46 Love is **weakened** when...
You start to envy the warm greetings and hugs your spouse gives to acquaintances.

47 Love is **weakened** when...
Your spouse plans a long vacation that does not include you.

48 Love is **weakened** when...
You get "stressed out" at work only to get "pushed out" at home.

49 Love is **weakened** when...
Your spouse feels that she "gave up her life" for you.

50 Love is **weakened** when...
Asking for a favor takes on an unpleasant flavor.

51 Love is **weakened** when...
You realize that all of your "mutual friends" are really just her friends.

52 Love is **weakened** when...
Gained wealth affords you the luxury of living apart.

53 Love is **weakened** when...
The successes and triumphs that once impressed your partner
now only distress her.

54 Love is **weakened** when…
You can no longer carry your spouse's premarital "hidden" baggage.

55 Love is **weakened** when…
You keep score.

56 Love is **weakened** when…
Your cats and dogs get warm hugs and kisses in the morning, and you don't.

57 Love is **weakened** when…
The only time you see the happy person you fell in love with is when your partner talks to others.

58 Love is **weakened** when…
Your spouse lets errors from one side of your character consume her whole vision of you.

59 Love is **weakened** when…
She gets flustered and angry when you come home early.

AGELESS RELATIONSHIP WISDOM

"We do not know what is good until we have lost it."
SPANISH PROVERB

"Every time you smile at someone, it is an action of love, a gift to that person, a beautiful thing."
MOTHER THERESA

60 Love is **weakened** when...
She seeks romantic love in the pages of a novel, yet shuns your touch.

61 Love is **weakened** when...
Your very being reminds your spouse of hurts from the past.

62 Love is **weakened** when...
Every waking moment is a reminder of something you "need to do" that will give you temporary freedom from your spouse.

63 Love is **weakened** when...
Terms of endearment are replaced with terms of disgust.

64 Love is **weakened** when...
Your most innocuous hobbies and interests start to infuriate your spouse.

65 Love is **weakened** when...
You get tired of saying, "My wife couldn't make it tonight."

66 Love is **weakened** when...
Your talents become laments in the eyes of your spouse.

67 Love is **weakened** when...
You wield your lover's confidences like daggers – weapons with which to reveal her secret weaknesses to the world.

68 Love is **weakened** when...
Phone-call silence becomes precious.

69 Love is **weakened** when...
Good deeds are never good enough.

70 Love is **weakened** when...
You lie about inconsequential things just to avoid a dramatic scene.

71 Love is **weakened** when...
Your partner criticizes your ideas, then takes the credit when they come to fruition.

72 Love is **weakened** when...
Your spouse expects you to have a crystal ball, but you are only human.

73 Love is **weakened** when...
Good-bye kisses are replaced by a wave from across the room.

74 Love is **weakened** when...
"Mr. Handyman" or "Mrs. Caregiver" gets taken for granted –
relied on but never appreciated.

75 Love is **weakened** when...
You are physically ill, and all your spouse can convey are feelings of dissatisfaction.

76 Love is **weakened** when...
Your spouse cannot say "thank you" without adding in some criticism
for good merit.

AGELESS RELATIONSHIP WISDOM

"Life without love is like a tree without blossom and fruit."
KHALIL GIBRAN

*"Seduce my mind and you can have my body;
find my soul and I'm yours forever."*
ANONYMOUS

77 Love is **weakened** when…
Money becomes an attractive tool to build barriers.

78 Love is **weakened** when…
You reminisce about past lovers and wonder if you took the right path.

79 Love is **weakened** when…
You have no time – or desire – to understand your lover's predicaments.

80 Love is **weakened** when…
"I dos" become "I won'ts."

81 Love is **weakened** when…
Your spouse has heartfelt conversations with her psychiatrist instead of you.

82 Love is **weakened** when…
Your separate bedroom becomes your refuge.

83 Love is **weakened** when…
You …

L oathe,
O verlook,
V oice disapproval of, and
E nvy

… Your partner.

84 Love is **weakened** when…
A simple "good morning" becomes an oxymoron.

85 Love is **weakened** when…
You find yourself sitting at opposite ends of the couch – or alone – every evening.

86 Love is **weakened** when…
There are not enough happy times to make the "work" worth the effort.

87 Love is **weakened** when…
Antipathy becomes your status quo.

88 Love is **weakened** when…
You begin to lie, first to your spouse and then to yourself.

89 Love is **weakened** when…
You do not consider your spouse worthy of tact and diplomacy.

90 Love is **weakened** when…
You force yourself to be cold and alienating.

91 Love is **weakened** when…
Your best friend no longer hears you.

92 Love is **weakened** when…
You no longer make time for each other.

AGELESS RELATIONSHIP WISDOM

"One word frees us of all the weight and pain in life;
that word is 'love.'"

SOCRATES

"Love teaches asses to dance."

FRENCH PROVERB

93 Love is **weakened** when...
Physical contact with your spouse makes you feel dirty.

94 Love is **weakened** when...
You expect your spouse to read your mind.

95 Love is **weakened** when...
You fear your spouse *wants* you to ask for a divorce.

96 Love is **weakened** when...
Simple "good nights" become a burden to utter.

97 Love is **weakened** when...
You don't keep your promises to one another.

98 Love is **weakened** when...
You conceal your naked body from the person who is intimately familiar with (and once turned on) by it.

99 Love is **weakened** when...
Your partner's goody drawer gets more action than you do.

100 Love is **weakened** when...
Morsels of kindness are met with immediate bitterness.

101 Love is **weakened** when...
You are so afraid of getting hurt that you hurt each other.

102 Love is **weakened** when...
You expect the present to change the past.

103 Love is **weakened** when...
You stop looking for the good in each other.

104 Love is **weakened** when…
You realize you've become self-destructive but are too proud to stop.

105 Love is **weakened** when…
You must filter the thoughts you once shared spontaneously.

106 Love is **weakened** when…
"I'm in the mood" becomes a dreaded invitation.

107 Love is **weakened** when…
The caresses that once made your heart race now make your stomach turn.

108 Love is **weakened** when…
You harshly judge the daydreams of your partner without considering their merits.

109 Love is **weakened** when…
You envy your partner's stray, innocent glances at others who exhibit the beauty you now hide from him.

110 Love is **weakened** when…
Your king-size bed has two layers of sheets: one level for him and one level for her.

AGELESS RELATIONSHIP WISDOM

"A kiss is a lovely trick designed by nature to stop speech when words become superfluous."

INGRID BERGMAN

"A heart that loves is always young."

GREEK PROVERB

111 Love is **weakened** when...

Your personal belongings are judged unfit or unattractive and get thrown away behind your back.

112 Love is **weakened** when...

You have no desire to spend time with your in-laws ... ever.

113 Love is **weakened** when...

Frequent written expressions of love are replaced with infrequent passé statements.

114 Love is **weakened** when...

Your honey loses his money – and suddenly seems less attractive.

115 Love is **weakened** when...

Your spouse dresses to impress at work and with friends – but adopts a Richard Simmons look-alike uniform at home.

116 Love is **weakened** when...

Your libido, once lauded, becomes a source of annoyance and strong criticism.

117 Love is **weakened** when...

Hugging your spouse feels like wrapping your arms around a statue.

118 Love is **weakened** when...

Gifts become expected but not appreciated.

119 Love is **weakened** when...

Absence does not make your heart grow fonder.

120 Love is **weakened** when...

Simple requests are constantly refused.

121 Love is **weakened** when…
Your sweetheart becomes a lemon sour.

122 Love is **weakened** when…
You have your own fan club, but your spouse is president of your "ban club."

123 Love is **weakened** when…
It seems simpler to have a one-night stand than to have one night of marital bliss.

124 Love is **weakened** when…
Everything that goes wrong is your fault.

125 Love is **weakened** when…
You stop making sexy invitations to avoid the pain of rejection.

126 Love is **weakened** when…
"I do love you" is followed up with a "but."

127 Love is **weakened** when…
Your spouse can accommodate functions for friends and your children, but not for you.

AGELESS RELATIONSHIP WISDOM

"Good manners are made up of petty sacrifices."

ANONYMOUS

*"Seldom, or perhaps never, does a marriage
develop into an individual relationship
smoothly and without crises; there is no coming
to consciousness without pain."*

CARL JUNG

128 Love is **weakened** when…
She has a million excuses for her absences.

129 Love is **weakened** when…
You wallow incessantly in past miseries.

130 Love is **weakened** when…
You expect your partner to like you while you debase her character to your family and friends.

131 Love is **weakened** when…
The balance of emotions and logic become skewed.

132 Love is **weakened** when…
The risks of life are too risky to be shared.

133 Love is **weakened** when…
Triumphs are shared joys and losses are her fault.

134 Love is **weakened** when…
The skirt of your love skirts your presence.

135 Love is **weakened** when…
You once threatened one another with tickles; now you threaten lawsuits.

136 Love is **weakened** when…
"Giving" is tantamount to being robbed.

137 Love is **weakened** when…
Your partner starts compulsively showering *every* time you finish making love.

138 Love is **weakened** when…
A meaningful relationship is truncated to a *mean* relationship.

139 Love is **weakened** when…
You cry alone – often.

140 Love is **weakened** when…
You treat love like a roller coaster instead of a Union Pacific long-haul train.

141 Love is **weakened** when…
Your heart feels as if it's been cryogenically frozen.

142 Love is **weakened** when…
You can no longer count your blessings with a straight face.

143 Love is **weakened** when…
You have to cry, "BELIEVE IN ME!"

144 Love is **weakened** when…
Friday date nights become Friday fight nights – and you begin to enjoy the sadomasochism of your knock-down-drag-outs.

145 Love is **weakened** when…
You're pretty sure that the grass is greener on the other side.

AGELESS RELATIONSHIP WISDOM

"A man of words and not of deeds is like
a garden full of weeds."
ANONYMOUS

"Married couples who love each other tell each
other a thousand things without talking."
CHINESE PROVERB

146 Love is **weakened** when...
The "elephants" fight and it is the "grass" (your children) that suffers.

147 Love is **weakened** when...
Sorrow can no longer be shared.

148 Love is **weakened** when...
You realize that you have journeyed down the wrong road but are too obstinate – or tired – to turn back.

149 Love is **weakened** when...
Laughter no longer matters.

150 Love is **weakened** when...
Marital spice is treated as marital lice.

151 Love is **weakened** when...
Complaints become more gratifying than solutions.

152 Love is **weakened** when...
Your spouse is the picture of grace, patience and courtesy – with everyone but you.

153 Love is **weakened** when...
You see only the thorns on the rose bush.

154 Love is **weakened** when...
You lead separate lives under the same roof.

155 Love is **weakened** when...
Housework becomes a four-letter word – one that rarely gets done.

156 Love is **weakened** when…
Your embrace is regarded as a restraint.

157 Love is **weakened** when…
You stop doing thoughtful things just to make your partner smile.

158 Love is **weakened** when…
You squelch the passions of your mate.

159 Love is **weakened** when…
You cease to see opportunities and possibilities.

160 Love is **weakened** when…
The impulse of your love no longer has a pulse.

161 Love is **weakened** when…
A greeting becomes a tepid meeting.

162 Love is **weakened** when…
Self-pity consumes your being.

AGELESS RELATIONSHIP WISDOM

*"The greatest tragedy of life is not that men
perish, but that they cease to love."*

W. SOMERSET MAUGHAM

*"Love is a passionate spiritual-emotional-sexual
attachment between a man and a woman that reflects
a high regard for the value of each other's person."*

NATHANIEL BRANDEN

163 Love is **weakened** when…
Honesty once strengthened your relationship; now it's a weapon that chips away at your bond.

164 Love is **weakened** when…
You lose your passion for a sense of justice in your marriage.

165 Love is **weakened** when…
You measure "I love you" on two very different scales.

166 Love is **weakened** when…
Your partner moves into a second home but still calls you her "spouse" and expects you to take care of all her needs … except one.

167 Love is **weakened** when…
The person you thought was your soul mate has you in checkmate.

168 Love is **weakened** when…
You use distorted truths to sway sympathies into your camp.

169 Love is **weakened** when…
"Spouse" and "friend" become mutually exclusive terms.

170 Love is **weakened** when…
You plan – and act – like you have no partner.

171 Love is **weakened** when…
You can't compromise without a lawyer present.

172 Love is **weakened** when…
Virtual (or fantasy) companionship with others replaces physical companionship with your partner.

173 Love is **weakened** when…
You yearn for attention your partner cannot give.

174 Love is **weakened** when…
You cannot agree on how to discipline and guide your children.

175 Love is **weakened** when…
Common-sense truths are distorted by personal "truths."

176 Love is **weakened** when…
You can recognize 103 facial expressions of dislike from your spouse.

177 Love is **weakened** when…
The heredity of your dysfunctional family becomes a dysfunctional reality in the family you created.

AGELESS RELATIONSHIP WISDOM

"Come live in my heart, and pay no rent."

SAMUEL LOVER

"Opposites attract, but after marriage, opposites attack. Unless you communicate, it's difficult to know how to love another person."

DR. CHARLES LOWERY

178 Love is **weakened** when...
You view your traits through a different lens than your partner.

Spouse's View   Your View

S mart
T alented
U nique
P layful
I ntrepid
D etermined

179 Love is **weakened** when...
You hold on to a grudge and will not budge.

180 Love is **weakened** when...
You tie the knot ... on your tubes, without informing your spouse.

181 Love is **weakened** when...
Your spouse is indifferent to your long work commute, as it means more free time for her.

182 Love is **weakened** when...
Your spouse employs the "power of the Lord" to prove his superiority.

183 Love is **weakened** when...
You feel you are in a perpetual state of loving the unlovely.

184 Love is **weakened** when...
Even your children wonder why you stay together.

185 Love is **weakened** when…
You make threats.

186 Love is **weakened** when…
Work is a sanctuary from home – where you derive the attention,
comfort and satisfaction you can't get from the one you love.

187 Love is **weakened** when…
You say hurtful things, knowing you'll wish you could take them back later.

189 Love is **weakened** when…
You conclude that some people should *never* be together.

190 Love is **weakened** when…
You feel your spouse thinks that *all* her troubles would go away if you did.

191 Love is **weakened** when…
He says "I love you" but no longer does anything to prove it.

192 Love is **weakened** when…
Silence is bliss, as it keeps you from getting pissed.

AGELESS RELATIONSHIP WISDOM

"In dreams and in love there are no impossibilities."

JANOS ARANY

*"Love withers with predictability; its very essence is
surprise and amazement. To make love a prisoner of the
mundane is to take its passion and lose it forever."*

LEO BUSCAGLIA

193 Love is **weakened** when…
You do the same things but expect different results.

194 Love is **weakened** when…
You live to be a martyr so God's grace and love can be with you.

195 Love is **weakened** when…
Time management involves spouse avoidance.

196 Love is **weakened** when…
Holding on to anger is more important than holding one another.

197 Love is **weakened** when…
Pretense for the sake of civility permeates your family life.

198 Love is **weakened** when…
You want your husband to have an affair so you can damn him.

199 Love is **weakened** when…
The fabric of your relationship is based upon fabricated stories.

200 Love is **weakened** when…
You take your BlackBerry to bed with you.

201 Love is **weakened** when…
The Middle East seems more peaceful than your home.

202 Love is **weakened** when…
Your partner is more loving with you in public than in private.

203 Love is **weakened** when…
Distrust necessitates stripping your spouse of all credit cards.

203 Love is **weakened** when…
You let your battle wounds make you into a recluse.

204 Love is **weakened** when…
Being absolutely right for the moment is more important than
being aligned on a long-term principle.

205 Love is **weakened** when…
You communicate via e-mail to avoid reading squirmy body language.

206 Love is **weakened** when…
Your spouse says your name like it's a four-letter word.

207 Love is **weakened** when…
A thousand counseling sessions and church sermons cannot squelch
your spouse's hatred.

208 Love is **weakened** when…
Simmering insults percolate unexpectedly.

AGELESS RELATIONSHIP WISDOM

"Patience is bitter but its fruit is sweet."
FRENCH PROVERB

*"The way I see it, if you want the rainbow,
you gotta put up with the rain."*
DOLLY PARTON

209 Love is **weakened** when...
You wish your life was as simple as a soap opera.

210 Love is **weakened** when...
You're not hot or cold – just numb and exhausted.

211 Love is **weakened** when...
You let depression become your master.

212 Love is **weakened** when...
You lose the desire to give your lover pleasure.

213 Love is **weakened** when...
You no longer have an intellectual connection.

214 Love is **weakened** when...
You are not cultured enough to appreciate your significant other's culture.

215 Love is **weakened** when...
Your spouse is nowhere near the top of your priority list.

216 Love is **weakened** when...
The sight of others in love makes you unhappy.

217 Love is **weakened** when...
You feel like a nobody when you are with your significant somebody.

218 Love is **weakened** when...
You lie or hide inconsequential things just for the sake of having secrets.

219 Love is **weakened** when…
Two people who once shared quaint moments begin to neglect instances of sweetness and closeness over time, until they morph into a couple of mere acquaintances.

220 Love is **weakened** when…
Rolling eyes stunt your rolling dialogue.

221 Love is **weakened** when…
You feel your place in your life's partnership is just claimed space.

222 Love is **weakened** when…
Your relationship boils down to one loooong argument!

223 Love is **weakened** when…
It seems less painful to swallow your own hurts than to share them with your loved one and risk being ridiculed.

224 Love is **weakened** when…
Your spouse lives with enduring penitence.

AGELESS RELATIONSHIP WISDOM

"Smile at each other, smile at your wife, smile at your husband, smile at your children, smile at each other – it doesn't matter who it is – and that will help you to grow up in greater love for each other."

MOTHER TERESA

"To say 'I love you,' one must first learn how to say the 'I.'"

AYN RAND

225 Love is **weakened** when...
You no longer try to spoil one another rotten.

226 Love is **weakened** when...
You are troubled by your relationship troubles every minute of every day.

227 Love is **weakened** when...
Your longing to be held fades away.

228 Love is **weakened** when...
You know to expect last-minute trinkets for presents on your birthday and anniversary.

229 Love is **weakened** when...
You are ridiculed for learning and sharing your knowledge.

230 Love is **weakened** when...
Your wife wants a constant "knight in shining armor," but you just need a respite.

231 Love is **weakened** when...
Your loved one has little zeal and follow-through for accomplishing anything, because he knows you will provide.

232 Love is **weakened** when...
Your spouse is a perpetual source of resistance.

233 Love is **weakened** when...
You realize that you are no longer playing on the same team – or even in the same league – as your partner.

234 Love is **weakened** when…
Your spouse has no time for loving, as constant commiserating
with others takes precedence.

235 Love is **weakened** when…
You prefer the companionship found in your company ship.

236 Love is **weakened** when…
You are willing to relinquish all worldly gains for a little peace,
with or without your mate.

237 Love is **weakened** when…
A wedding band locks you into a perpetuity of servitude instead
of a partnership for eternity.

238 Love is **weakened** when…
You realize that caller ID helps your spouse ignore your calls.

239 Love is **weakened** when…
Your relationship is divided by separate "religionships."

AGELESS RELATIONSHIP WISDOM

*"A man falls in love through his eyes,
a woman through her ears."*
WOODROW WYATT

*"Courage, love, friendship, compassion and empathy lift
us above the simple beasts and define humanity."*
THE BOOK OF COUNTED SORROWS

240 Love is **weakened** when...
Loose emotions are mistaken for high emotional intelligence.

241 Love is **weakened** when...
You live in an irreparably broken home and don't leave.

242 Love is **weakened** when...
Your spouse fabricates woes in a psychosomatic fashion.

243 Love is **weakened** when...
Your spouse's attorney has identified how much you are worth.

244 Love is **weakened** when...
Compromise becomes as elusive as your sex life.

245 Love is **weakened** when...
Intimacy (into-me-u-c) becomes too revealing, so you build walls to ward off the pain.

246 Love is **weakened** when...
The need for miserly practices (like canceling date night) leads to misery.

247 Love is **weakened** when...
Marital integration spoils into disintegration.

248 Love is **weakened** when...
Your partner acts so independently of you that you feel forgotten, like a relic of the past.

249 Love is **weakened** when...
Sarcasm becomes the only form of "humor" in your relationship.

250 Love is **weakened** when…
Your marriage is based on duty and honor, absent any passion.

251 Love is **weakened** when…
You are needed but not wanted.

252 Love is **weakened** when…
Your partner reaps the reward in times of plenty and blames you
in times of scarcity.

253 Love is **weakened** when…
Your spouse is scared to be with you and scared to be without you.

254 Love is **weakened** when…
The music keeps playing, but your spouse has tuned you out.

255 Love is **weakened** when…
Bitter digs replace sweet nothings.

256 Love is **weakened** when…
You no longer care enough to comfort one another.

AGELESS RELATIONSHIP WISDOM

*"The best portion of a good man's life – his little nameless,
unremembered acts of kindness and love."*

WILLIAM WORDSWORTH

*"One can live magnificently in this world if one
knows how to work and how to love."*

LEO TOLSTOY

257 Love is **weakened** when...
Midday calls, texts or e-mails just to say "hi" seem absurd.

258 Love is **weakened** when...
You find yourself sleeping with the enemy.

259 Love is **weakened** when...
Your partner doesn't mind if you're around or if you're not.

260 Love is **weakened** when...
The dance you crave to share with your spouse is now a daily tug-of-war.

261 Love is **weakened** when...
Mean-spirited telephone conversations prove a new physical law:
that pointed daggers can travel via wireless signal.

262 Love is **weakened** when...
Your partner starts yelling before you finish explaining.

263 Love is **weakened** when...
You're not "allowed" to spend time with your friends and family.

264 Love is **weakened** when...
You keep lowering the bar of expectations until you can't even see it anymore.

265 Love is **weakened** when...
You become a scapegoat, and your spouse is eager to set you free.

266 Love is **weakened** when...
You watch movies with your spouse, and the sex scenes make you uncomfortable
– even though you once acted out your own X-rated scenes together.

267 Love is **weakened** when...
You get so bored with your life that you start to understand why some people marry much younger women or much older men.

268 Love is **weakened** when...
Your partner "lets herself go" and doesn't understand why it bothers you.

269 Love is **weakened** when...
Every communication with the opposite sex is misinterpreted by your spouse as an expression of lustful intentions.

270 Love is **weakened** when...
You fail to realize that the wings of ecstasy also need landing gear.

271 Love is **weakened** when...
Having a discussion becomes a surgically-precise exercise to minimize collateral dialogue, instead of an open forum to explore life's beauty.

272 Love is **weakened** when...
Books or TV become better company than your spouse and are your only relief from the persistent loneliness.

AGELESS RELATIONSHIP WISDOM

"The greatest gift is a portion of thyself."

RALPH WALDO EMERSON

"You never lose by loving. You only lose by holding back."

BARBARA DE ANGELIS

273 Love is **weakened** when...
You tear apart your partner's dreams and convince yourself that you're just offering sound advice.

274 Love is **weakened** when...
You feel there is nothing left to lose.

275 Love is **weakened** when...
Your books, your music and your thoughts are insulted.

276 Love is **weakened** when...
You refuse to hone your own skills but mock those who live their own dreams.

277 Love is **weakened** when...
Your spouse complains that you do not share your feelings, but tunes you out or argues with you when you try.

278 Love is **weakened** when...
Your sexual fantasies *never* involve your spouse.

279 Love is **weakened** when...
Your Wonderbra entices the crowd, but your husband knows it wasn't worn to entice *him*.

280 Love is **weakened** when...
Your spouse resents the fact that you make more money.

281 Love is **weakened** when...
You make a mortgage payment more often than you have sex.

282 Love is **weakened** when...
Talking to your partner about anything is too much work.

283 Love is **weakened** when…
A part of you dies, and your partner doesn't even notice.

284 Love is **weakened** when…
The laughter stops.

285 Love is **weakened** when…
You consider having an affair just to feel alive again.

286 Love is **weakened** when…
Staying with your partner is scarier than the unknown of leaving
and starting all over again *alone*.

287 Love is **weakened** when…
You are in a crisis, and the last person you want to lean on is your partner.

288 Love is **weakened** when…
There is no more love in your lovemaking.

289 Love is **weakened** when…
You hope your partner does something bad enough that you *have* to leave.

AGELESS RELATIONSHIP WISDOM

*"The greatest happiness of life is the conviction
that we are all loved."*

VICTOR HUGO

*"It is not the perfect but the imperfect
who need to be loved."*

EDITH WHARTON

290 Love is **weakened** when...
Your partner's presence is no longer a present.

291 Love is **weakened** when...
You stop sharing about your life with your friends and family for fear they will know how broken your home really is.

292 Love is **weakened** when...
You fear the mirror, because it reminds you that you're not sure who you are anymore.

293 Love is **weakened** when...
Even the easy times and simple tasks in your life feel hard.

294 Love is **weakened** when...
You stop living and start just existing.

295 Love is **weakened** when...
You stop wearing your wedding rings.

296 Love is **weakened** when...
Your wife says your daughter will live a life of pain because her boyfriend is just like you.

297 Love is **weakened** when...
You stop telling new acquaintances that you are married.

298 Love is **weakened** when...
You start comparing your relationship to everyone else's – and are pretty sure you've drawn the shortest stick.

299 Love is **weakened** when…
You have nothing left to give – and you no longer expect anything
from your partner.

300 Love is **weakened** when…
You fantasize about what your life would be like without your spouse.

301 Love is **weakened** when…
There is no benefit of a doubt.

302 Love is **weakened** when…
You are jealous of friends who are already divorced.

303 Love is **weakened** when…
You only initiate sex when it occurs to you that it's been a while and
you know it's something you're "supposed" to do in a relationship.

304 Love is **weakened** when…
You can no longer have dinner together without the TV or some other
distraction.

AGELESS RELATIONSHIP WISDOM

"If you judge people, you have no time left to love them."
MOTHER TERESA

*"Truly loving another means letting go of all
expectations. It means full acceptance, even
celebration of another's personhood."*
KAREN CASEY

305 Love is **weakened** when...
Your routine becomes so routine that you don't have to speak to each other to get through it.

306 Love is **weakened** when...
It becomes hard to remember the happy, special moments you once shared.

307 Love is **weakened** when...
Even "hope" seems like a four-letter word.

308 Love is **weakened** when...
You stop looking for a way back in and start thinking about the way out.

309 Love is **weakened** when...
The idea of any family activity becomes daunting.

310 Love is **weakened** when...
You stop taking family photos because no one wants to be in them.

311 Love is **weakened** when...
Having a baby to make things better seems like a good idea.

312 Love is **weakened** when...
You want to run away.

313 Love is **weakened** when...
The solutions to make things better overwhelm instead of excite you.

314 Love is **weakened** when...
Your children ask why Mommy and Daddy no longer sleep together, eat meals together, smile at one another or spend alone time together.

315 Love is **weakened** when...

You start taking your frustration out on the cat and drive-thru attendants.

316 Love is **weakened** when...

Your spouse plans her errands when she knows you're on the way home so she can prolong the day's separation.

317 Love is **weakened** when...

His messy habits (like dirty socks on the floor) infuriate you, when you used to just laugh and pick them up.

318 Love is **weakened** when...

Seeing your spouse play with your children makes you jealous and annoyed, when it used to make your heart flutter.

319 Love is **weakened** when...

You start getting jealous and insecure about things that never bothered you before.

AGELESS RELATIONSHIP WISDOM

"If you press me to say why I loved him, I can say no more than because he was he and I was I."

MICHAEL DE MONTAIGNE

"That you may be loved, be loveable."

OVID

320 Love is **weakened** when...
You don't want your spouse to meet your new friends, simply because you don't want to share that part of your life.

321 Love is **weakened** when...
You accidentally-on-purpose fall asleep on the couch to avoid sleeping with your spouse.

322 Love is **weakened** when...
You start rolling your eyes and sighing without even realizing you're doing it.

323 Love is **weakened** when...
You only say "I love you" because you realize you haven't said it in weeks.

324 Love is **weakened** when...
You start snooping through your partner's e-mail and phone records.

325 Love is **weakened** when...
You consider calling up his ex to compare notes and ask what went wrong in their relationship.

326 Love is **weakened** when...
You take more comfort in the bitterness you are experiencing than in the possible ways you could make things better, because hey, it's the devil that you know.

327 Love is **weakened** when...
You truly believe that *all* your relationship problems are your spouse's fault and that there's nothing *you* need to work on.

328 Love is **weakened** when...
You stop fighting – because you stop talking altogether.

329 Love is **weakened** when…
Sharing a toothbrush or towel with your spouse now nauseates you, though it used to make you feel close.

330 Love is **weakened** when…
You make major decisions without even asking your partner's opinion.

331 Love is **weakened** when…
Your spouse wants to change you – or gets mad because you change.

332 Love is **weakened** when…
You can't remember the last time your spouse complimented you.

333 Love is **weakened** when…
You cry quietly after your partner falls asleep, because talking about it hasn't worked in the past.

334 Love is **weakened** when…
You spend all your time thinking, "What if?"

AGELESS RELATIONSHIP WISDOM

"Love sought is good; love unsought is even better."

SHAKESPEARE

"This fundamental truth – that woman are not just men who can have babies and men are not just women who spike footballs – gives marriage its vitality, its dynamics and its delights."

BILL COSBY

335 Love is **weakened** when...
Your husband looks at other women the way he used to look at you.

336 Love is **weakened** when...
You enjoy hearing others talk about problems in their relationships because it makes you feel less lonely – and more vindicated.

337 Love is **weakened** when...
You take the family photo off your desk so you won't have to fake marital bliss when new clients ask about it.

338 Love is **weakened** when...
You start separating your finances after years of joint checking.

339 Love is **weakened** when...
You start wishing there weren't so many potential weapons lying around your house, because you worry you might use them.

340 Love is **weakened** when...
You live your life as if the glass is always half empty.

341 Love is **weakened** when...
You no longer have "make-up sex" after heated arguments.

342 Love is **weakened** when...
You spend hours in the same room and never even make eye contact.

343 Love is **weakened** when...
You stop looking at pictures from the beginning of the relationship so you don't see how far you have fallen.

344 Love is **weakened** when...
You once left love notes for each other to find; now you leave to-do lists.

345 Love is **weakened** when…
Your spouse is so bored and depressed that she puts you in debt
with shopping therapy.

346 Love is **weakened** when…
You stop shaving to keep your spouse's advances at bay.

347 Love is **weakened** when…
You pretend to fall asleep so you don't have to listen to your spouse
talk about his day.

348 Love is **weakened** when…
You have to tell yourself, "It will be over soon," to get through sex with
your partner.

349 Love is **weakened** when…
You sleep with a body but snuggle with your pillow.

350 Love is **weakened** when…
You don't feel that you spend enough time with your mate.

AGELESS RELATIONSHIP WISDOM

*"Love is a sweet tyranny, because the lover
endureth his torments willingly."*

PROVERB

*"The lover is a monotheist who knows that other
people worship different gods but cannot himself
imagine that there could be other gods."*

THEODOR REIK

351 Love is **weakened** when...
Revenge feels sweet; kindness, bitter.

352 Love is **weakened** when...
You focus on the 20 percent of your union that is not perfect and destroy the 80 percent that is.

353 Love is **weakened** when...
Your batteries need a recharge; you get physical battery instead.

354 Love is **weakened** when...
You watch the one you love, love someone else.

355 Love is **weakened** when...
You discover love, yet do not know what to do with it.

356 Love is **weakened** when...
Your heartbreak causes your body to break down too.

357 Love is **weakened** when...
You are no longer your soul mate's sole mate.

358 Love is **weakened** when...
The power of love is merely a love of power.

359 Love is **weakened** when...
Your reflexes are abrupt; your reflections, nonexistent.

360 Love is **weakened** when...
You realize you wasted your life trying to find the perfect lover, instead of creating a perfect love with an imperfect person.

361 Love is **weakened** when…
Your friends "disappear" because they can no longer condone your relationship.

362 Love is **weakened** when…
Your partner has no idea who the real you is.

363 Love is **weakened** when…
The person you thought you loved molds and shapes you into someone you loathe.

364 Love is **weakened** when…
Your exes are living ghosts in your present relationship.

365 Love is **weakened** when…
The triumphant twang of the bedspring has gone dormant.

366 Love is **weakened** when…
You cannot experience joy because you live in sadness, and you cannot see the light because you live in darkness.

AGELESS RELATIONSHIP WISDOM

"The sight of lovers feedeth those in love."
SHAKESPEARE

"Love is the only sane and satisfactory answer to the problem of human existence."
ERICH FROMM

367 Love is **weakened** when...
You strive to love your children while you hate their other parent.

368 Love is **weakened** when...
You do not feel good about yourself.

369 Love is **weakened** when...
You suppress the light that shines on the beauty of your partner's soul.

370 Love is **weakened** when...
The skeletons in your closet threaten to send your love to the grave.

371 Love is **weakened** when...
Resolutions have no resolution.

372 Love is **weakened** when...
You use people and love things.

373 Love is **weakened** when...
You work for the love of money.

374 Love is **weakened** when...
Your home is a dictatorship.

375 Love is **weakened** when...
You live with a self-professed "professional critic."

376 Love is **weakened** when...
Your mate cannot allow herself to be loved.

377 Love is **weakened** when...
You treat your relationship like a one-way street.

378 Love is **weakened** when...
Personal satisfaction trumps mutual satisfaction.

379 Love is **weakened** when...
You cannot utter three simple words: "I love you."

380 Love is **weakened** when...
You don't say how you feel until it's too late.

381 Love is **weakened** when...
You force love from your love before hers has ripened.

382 Love is **weakened** when...
Only one partner grows.

383 Love is **weakened** when...
You seek to possess rather than to trust.

384 Love is **weakened** when...
You don't make each other better and stronger.

AGELESS RELATIONSHIP WISDOM

"Love is an act of endless forgiveness,
a tender look which becomes a habit."
PETER USTINOV

"Hate leaves ugly scars, love leaves beautiful ones."
MIGNON MCLAUGHLIN

385 Love is **weakened** when…
Your partner loves who he wants you to be, not who you are.

386 Love is **weakened** when…
You are dissected wholeheartedly and without compassion.

387 Love is **weakened** when…
Affection has a price.

388 Love is **weakened** when…
Your words speak of love, but your deeds do not.

389 Love is **weakened** when…
You constantly neglect your own needs.

390 Love is **weakened** when…
Arrogance squelches the love of your partner.

391 Love is **weakened** when…
You are too lazy to create the life you yearn to live.

392 Love is **weakened** when…
You believe conniving can bring you love.

393 Love is **weakened** when…
Your heart beats for that someone special, who beats you into submission.

394 Love is **weakened** when…
Your loneliness never goes away.

395 Love is **weakened** when…
You let your partner down all the time.

396 Love is **weakened** when…
You risk nothing for love, and therefore risk everything.

397 Love is **weakened** when…
You only want what you can't have.

398 Love is **weakened** when…
The connections between your bodies do not mirror the connections between your minds, hearts and souls.

399 Love is **weakened** when…
The one who loves least is the one who controls the relationship.

400 Love is **weakened** when…
You are constantly up in arms instead of being in each other's arms.

401 Love is **weakened** when…
You can identify with too many of these in your current relationship.

AGELESS RELATIONSHIP WISDOM

"Love looks not with the eyes, but with the mind,
and therefore is winged Cupid painted blind."

WILLIAM SHAKESPEARE

"The art of love is largely the art of persistence."

ALBERT ELLIS

USE THIS SPACE TO WRITE ABOUT HOW YOU
FEEL LOVE IS LOST IN YOUR RELATIONSHIP

USE THIS SPACE TO WRITE ABOUT HOW YOU
FEEL LOVE IS LOST IN YOUR RELATIONSHIP

Do you have suggestions for other ways love is weakened that you would like to share
for future editions? Please e-mail them for consideration to **loveisweakened@loveislost.com**.
(See submission terms at the back of this book.)

"Love is a temporary madness. It erupts like an earthquake and then subsides. And when it subsides you have to make a decision. You have to work out whether your roots have become so entwined together that it is inconceivable that you should ever part. Because this is what love is. Love is not breathlessness, it is not excitement, it is not the promulgation of promises of eternal passion. That is just being 'in love,' which any of us can convince ourselves we are. Love itself is what is left over when being in love has burned away, and this is both an art and a fortunate accident. Your mother and I had it, we had roots that grew towards each other underground, and when all the pretty blossom had fallen from our branches we found that we were one tree and not two."

ST. AUGUSTINE
Shared in the movie *Captain Corelli's Mandolin*

—SECTION 2—
LOVE IS
FELT WHEN...

What are the feelings and emotions that envelop love? How do we know when we are in love? What do our partners do that makes us feel loved? How do we know that Cupid's arrow has struck and that this time, it is the real thing?

There are a million and one possible ways that enamored couples demonstrate their love for each other. Some of these pleasures of the soul will ebb and flow in a relationship, depending on the circumstances, but they persist over time. Sure, some ways that we say "I love you" (even the act of saying "I love you") may depend, in large part, on our personalities and our upbringings. But many of these indicators cross the boundaries of personality types and cultures. They are, in essence, the foundations on which relationships are built.

When the core values of a couple are in alignment, love is a many-splendored thing. Here are some ways to show your lover that you love her (or him). Look for these in your relationship, and if they're not there, find ways to imbue some of them into your union.

1 Love is felt when...

You are just as excited to see the goals of your loved one materialize
as you are to see your own.

2 Love is felt when...

You feel comfort and support from him in the midst of a crisis, even when
it feels like everything (and everyone) else is working against you.

3 Love is felt when...

You can express your innermost fears and thoughts without fear of
rejection or ridicule.

4 Love is felt when...

You understand your partner so well that sometimes words aren't necessary,
and peace is relatively easy.

5 Love is felt when...

After an extended period of separation, you get butterflies in your
stomach and blush with excitement to see each other.

6 Love is **felt** when…
You can imagine the worst day of your life and know it will be
better and easier with him beside you.

7 Love is **felt** when…
You can hear what your love is saying, even if it is hard or painful.

8 Love is **felt** when…
You are proud to stand next to him, even in his darkest moment.

9 Love is **felt** when…
You tremble at the anticipation of his touch.

10 Love is **felt** when…
There is gentleness between you, even after years of tough times.

11 Love is **felt** when…
You realize that the quality of your life will never be the same without her.

AGELESS RELATIONSHIP WISDOM

"Love must be as much a light, as it is a flame."
HENRY DAVID THOREAU

*"To find someone who will love you for no reason,
and to shower that person with reasons,
that is the ultimate happiness."*
ROBERT BRAULT

12 Love is **felt** when...
You can feel his pain and want nothing more than to ease it and make the situation better.

13 Love is **felt** when...
You offer her your world, still wishing you had more to give.

14 Love is **felt** when...
You want him to hold your hair back while you're sick – even though you know you look like the living dead.

15 Love is **felt** when...
A simple kiss on the hand or forehead makes your heart melt.

16 Love is **felt** when...
Making love is another way to share your heart, soul and intentions.

17 Love is **felt** when...
You share the same dreams, even if they are on a different timetable.

18 Love is **felt** when...
You want more for him than you want for yourself.

19 Love is **felt** when...
There is no room for jealousy and insecurity.

20 Love is **felt** when...
You come together and create one life but find ways to enjoy your independence.

21 Love is **felt** when...
You feel as intimate and connected when you are apart as you do when you are together.

22 Love is **felt** when...
Other people tell you that you're so cute together, you make them sick
(but they're smiling when they say it).

23 Love is **felt** when...
You respect and trust one another.

24 Love is **felt** when...
You say "thank you," even for tasks your partner is "supposed" to do.

25 Love is **felt** when...
You don't consider your efforts to help one another's dreams
come true "sacrifices."

26 Love is **felt** when...
You two speak a language that no one else knows – and you can
do it without words.

27 Love is **felt** when...
The way you dance together signifies to the whole world that
you are in perfect unison.

AGELESS RELATIONSHIP WISDOM

*"Love one another and you will be happy.
It's as simple and as difficult as that."*
MICHAEL LEUNIG

*"Love is the condition in which the happiness of
another person is essential to your own."*
ROBERT HEINLEIN

28 Love is felt when...
Your relationship is so healthy, you can spend time nourishing your relationships with others without taking away from your time together.

29 Love is felt when...
Everyday tasks can be just as sensual as an evening alone in bed.

30 Love is felt when...
You define and value unyielding commitment the same way.

31 Love is felt when...
You *love* to watch others in love and revel in their happiness.

32 Love is felt when...
The tone of your voice and the look on your face change just for him.

33 Love is felt when...
You have shared interests and solo hobbies – and you encourage each other to experience both.

34 Love is felt when...
You trust him as much as you trust yourself.

35 Love is felt when...
You call or e-mail to check in during the day, just because you're thinking about her.

36 Love is felt when...
You can still talk for hours when the mood strikes.

37 Love is felt when...
You ask for his opinion even when you don't have to.

38 Love is **felt** when…
You genuinely care how her day was.

39 Love is **felt** when…
You're proud to introduce her to your friends – new and old.

40 Love is **felt** when…
You parent as a team – a unified front.

41 Love is **felt** when…
You offer feedback without criticizing.

42 Love is **felt** when…
You take comfort in going to bed at night and waking up in
your loved one's arms.

43 Love is **felt** when…
You find yourself smiling spontaneously when he crosses your mind.

44 Love is **felt** when…
You know without a doubt that she has your best interests at heart.

AGELESS RELATIONSHIP WISDOM

"Only in love are unity and duality not in conflict."
RABINDRANATH TAGORE

*"When you're attracted to someone, it just means that
your subconscious is attracted to their subconscious,
subconsciously, so what we know as fate is two neuroses
knowing that they're a perfect match."*

JEFF ARCH, NORA EPHRON, AND DAVID S. WARD,
SLEEPLESS IN SEATTLE

61

45 Love is felt when...
You want to share everything with your loved one.

46 Love is felt when...
You look forward to lazy Sunday mornings when you can just cuddle and spend quality time with your partner.

47 Love is felt when...
Long car trips and delayed flights aren't so bad – as long as your copilot is along for the ride.

48 Love is felt when...
You suddenly feel more relaxed just because he entered the room.

49 Love is felt when...
You celebrate your partner's accomplishments as much as or more than your own.

50 Love is felt when...
You share jokes no one else understands.

51 Love is felt when...
You both do your part for the team, but no one keeps score.

52 Love is felt when...
You are kind even when you don't want to be.

53 Love is felt when...
You know your partner would rather be with you than with anyone else in the world.

54 Love is felt when...
Your spouse makes your life more peaceful and joyful – at least most of the time.

55 Love is **felt** when…

You take the time to learn each other's needs (physical desires, communication and deeds).

56 Love is **felt** when…

You accept the real differences between the sexes (and between individuals) and learn how to handle moods, stress, work and life's peculiarities instead of trying to change your mate.

57 Love is **felt** when…

You hug and kiss whenever you can – for the sake of your emotional bond and your physical one.

50 Love is **felt** when…

You NEVER say anything emotionally damaging to the other person in front of others.

AGELESS RELATIONSHIP WISDOM

"We waste time looking for the perfect lover,
instead of creating the perfect love."

TOM ROBBINS

"We are not the same persons this year as last; nor
are those we love. It is a happy chance if we, changing,
continue to love a changed person."

W. SOMERSET MAUGHAM

USE THIS SPACE TO WRITE ABOUT HOW YOU
FEEL LOVE IS FELT IN YOUR RELATIONSHIP

USE THIS SPACE TO WRITE ABOUT HOW YOU
FEEL LOVE IS FELT IN YOUR RELATIONSHIP

Do you have suggestions for other ways love is felt that you would like to share
for future editions? Please e-mail them for consideration to **loveisfelt@loveislost.com**.
(See submission terms at the back of this book.)

"Married couples who love each other tell each other a thousand things without talking."

CHINESE PROVERB

"One word frees us of all the weight and pain in life; that word is 'love.'"

SOCRATES

—SECTION 3—
LOVE IS REIGNITED WHEN...

When two lovers first meet, the stars align in the heavens. When they first kiss, the sparks fly. And when Cupid really hits his mark, they take some vows and hope for a happily ever after.

Then comes reality. After a few years together, once routines have been formed, interesting stories have all been told, crises have been experienced and unflattering sides of our character have been revealed, the connection that once made hearts flutter can get muted – by busy schedules, other people, drugs or alcohol, or even just emotional distance.

Many long-standing relationships never make it to the altar. Half of those that do end in divorce, and many others just bear the frustration or apathy and stay in unhappy marriages.

If your relationship is in a tense, angry, cold or just boring place, it is within your power to change the tide, to rekindle the connection that brought you together in the first place and build a relationship that breeds understanding, nurtures empathy, strengthens character and achieves real happiness. Or, at the very least (if things are, in fact, irreparably broken), you will know that you have done everything you could to reignite the love before you walked away.

This section lists ways to replenish and nourish the emotional bonds – the closeness, the friendship and the sexual connection – that hold your relationship together. Whether your relationship is in trouble or you want to keep it (or the next one) *out* of trouble, know that once the emotional connection is established – and every time it is strengthened – the physical and spiritual bonds will inevitably become stronger.

Just remember that, at the end of the day, you and your partner are two very unique and special individuals, but neither of you are – or will be – perfect. A pastor by the name of Jay Pankratz, whose church I (Enrique) used to attend in Southern California, frequently shared the story of a couple he knew who had been married for 50-plus years. When others asked the wife how she kept her marriage strong for all those years, she would say, "When we got married, I realized that my husband had eight qualities I was not thrilled about, but I decided that I would learn to accept those things in our marriage because, everything else was great." When someone asked her what those eight qualities were, she answered, "I don't know. I just know that when he does something that annoys me, it is one of those eight things. And I move on, because it is one of those things I agreed to accept." Bravo, lady! The secret to a happy marriage between two imperfect people who love more about each other than they dislike: focus on the 80 or so percent of your relationship that bonds your souls!

1 Love is **reignited** when...

You schedule a weekly date night and make it your No. 1 priority.

2 Love is **reignited** when...

You improve your communication skills. (Resolve to stop interrupting or getting angry at the beginning of a conversation and to hear your partner out before you jump to conclusions.)

3 Love is **reignited** when...

You go an entire week without criticizing your partner. (At the end of the week, think about the things that upset you most, that most made you want to react, and forget about everything else. In other words, learn to pick your battles.)

4 Love is **reignited** when...

You turn off the BlackBerry, TV and computer at least an hour before bed (and for whole evenings whenever possible) and just focus on one another.

5 Love is **reignited** when...

You go away for a weekend together, or get your parents to keep the children overnight, so you can have some grown-ups-only time.

AGELESS RELATIONSHIP WISDOM

"Love is missing someone whenever you're apart, but somehow feeling warm inside because you're close in heart."

URSULA K. LEGUIN

"A good marriage is one which allows for change and growth in the individuals and in the way they express their love."

PEARL S. BUCK

6 Love is reignited when...

You talk about your problems when you're *not* angry. (Rather than waiting until you're in mid-fight, talk about the issue when you're both calm. If your discussions tend to get tense, try writing down what you want to say to one another, sleeping on it for a night and then revising the next day. Limit your anger and blame, and instead focus on how you *feel* when your partner does XYZ. Once you feel good about what you've written, exchange letters and give each other at least a day to consider your points, get past the immediate emotions and formulate a response. *Then* talk about it.)

7 Love is reignited when...

You choose a TV show that you'd both like to watch (either via a weekly broadcast or on DVD) and schedule a regular night to enjoy watching together. Or read the same book at the same time and discuss it. (If nothing else, it's quiet time together, and the shared experience will give you something to talk about.)

8 Love is reignited when...

You spice things up in the bedroom. (Share your fantasies and try something new, like a sexy board game, dressing up or role-playing – something out of the ordinary that excites your partner and won't make you too uncomfortable. Just making the effort will make things better.)

9 Love is reignited when...

You take up a hobby together. (Whether it's cooking lessons, tennis or scuba diving, try something you've both always wanted to do but haven't.)

10 Love is reignited when...

You remember what first attracted you to your partner. (Then think about what you could do that would rekindle those qualities in your mate. For example, if you loved how she always seemed excited to see you walk in the door, surprise her by bringing home her favorite flowers or something thoughtful that would make her smile. Or if you liked the fact that he was adventurous, plan a hiking trip.)

11 Love is **reignited** when...

You dress up. (Sure, sweatpants, ponytails and five o'clock shadows are more comfortable, and it's nice to be comfy at home. But occasionally, put as much effort into looking good at home as you do into going out. And that goes for men as well as women.)

12 Love is **reignited** when...

You capitalize on any opportunity (like long car trips or flights with your partner) to catch up on the missed moments of your busy lives.

13 Love is **reignited** when...

You let him be him, and he lets you be you, believing things will fall into place with patience, faith and compassion.

14 Love is **reignited** when...

You believe and trust in love.

15 Love is **reignited** when...

You choose your words carefully, even when you're angry. (Put thought into how your message is being received, and deliver it with as much compassion and tenderness as possible, knowing that once the words leave your mouth, they can't ever go back.)

AGELESS RELATIONSHIP WISDOM

"Love doesn't sit there like a stone, it has to be made, like bread; remade all of the time, made new."

KAY KNUDSEN

"Women marry men hoping they will change. Men marry women hoping they will not. So each is inevitably disappointed."

ALBERT EINSTEIN

16 Love is reignited when...
You forgive. (If you keep prosecuting each other for the same crimes, you'll never move forward.)

17 Love is reignited when...
You don't expect your loved one to be your everything for every minute of every day, and you accept that you cannot be his.

18 Love is reignited when...
You both put the good of the team in front of your individual needs. (If you're both working toward a common goal, there's no need to keep score. Compromises all even out in the wash.)

19 Love is reignited when...
You accept that your relationship is a work in progress but agree to do your share of the growing.

20 Love is reignited when...
You try to understand where she's coming from, even when you disagree.

21 Love is reignited when...
You take five minutes out of every day to write in a journal the things that you appreciated about your mate on that particular day – anything from the way she fixed her hair or the work he did on the car, to the meal she prepared for you or the good-morning kiss he gave you. (It's easy to start taking one another for granted after a while. This practice keeps you focused on everything you have to appreciate in your partner, and makes a thoughtful gift to share at Thanksgiving.)

22 Love is reignited when...
You can be honest with yourself and take the time for self-examination. (When you can see yourself clearly – your strengths *and* weaknesses, your needs and limits – you will be in a better position to communicate with each other.)

23 Love is **reignited** when...

You do something, or some things, that are unpredictable! (Our everyday routines are our routines because they work for us, but stepping out of the ordinary and taking it up a notch, at least every once in a while, goes a long way toward keeping your relationship feeling fresh and exciting.)

24 Love is **reignited** when...

You can be responsive to each other's needs and wants, even when those requests seem trivial to you. (Better yet, don't wait until your partner asks. Go out of your way to anticipate small favors that would make your loved one happy.)

25 Love is **reignited** when...

You put your relationship first! (Sure, everyone and everything – from your job, to your house, to your children – needs your time and attention, but it will all suffer in one shape or form if you don't take care of your relationship first.)

26 Love is **reignited** when...

You take care of yourself. (You will have more to offer your loved one if you stop to refuel from time to time. Don't put yourself on the bottom of your priority list. Take some time for yourself, and enjoy it.)

AGELESS RELATIONSHIP WISDOM

*"Anyone can be passionate,
but it takes real lovers to be silly."*

ROSE FRANKEN

*"Happy marriages begin when we marry the ones we love,
and they blossom when we love the ones we marry."*

TOM MULLEN

27 Love is reignited when...

You can look at the big picture. (Instead of focusing on the little things that annoy you about each other – like how he laughs or the way she bites her nails – examine what you love about your partner, where you have been and where you want to be, and why you want to get there together.)

28 Love is reignited when...

You recognize that forgiveness is essential to healing a broken relationship, and that holding on to hurt and anger will only drive you crazy and ruin the relationship in the long run. Two critical keys to forgiveness are:

1) Understanding your pain by fully examining its cause and how you may be expressing it.

2) Taking responsibility for your pain and anger and making the effort to communicate about it with your loved one.

29 Love is reignited when...

You communicate often and about everything. (Begin to examine each other's hopes, dreams and goals, and use detail when talking about them. Why are they important? What will it mean to each of you if one or both of you accomplishes each goal? This type of sharing can lead to a feeling of intimacy that just belongs to the two of you.)

30 Love is reignited when...

You let go of fear. (Worrying about getting hurt will only keep you from experiencing the connection you truly want. Look closely at the cause of that fear and then release it. Imagine the worst-case scenario, and then acknowledge that whatever it is wouldn't break you. Why love halfway if you can afford the possible price of loving the way you want?)

31 Love is reignited when…

You strive to be gentle and kind with your words when communicating with your loved one. If what you are saying is not being received the way you need it to be, then try again, putting some thought into what you want your partner to hear.

32 Love is reignited when…

You take action to live a healthier lifestyle today so you can be there for more of your partner's tomorrows. (Showing that you care about how your decisions affect your partner – or better yet, deciding to exercise and eat more healthfully together – speaks volumes about your commitment to a life together.)

33 Love is reignited when…

You realize that your body language – like rolled eyes, crossed arms, heavy sighs and other defensive postures – communicates more than words alone and can, in fact, cancel out what you *say*. (It has been said that the way a person interprets what we say in a phone conversation is based 80 percent on tone and 20 percent on words. In person, 55 percent of a message is communicated non-verbally, 38 percent by how you say it and only 7 percent by what you actually say. So being aware of your body language, tone and presentation – making sure they are actually communicating the message you intend – can save you worlds of hurt due to misunderstanding.)

AGELESS RELATIONSHIP WISDOM

"Marriage is not a noun; it's a verb. It isn't something you get. It's something you do. It's the way you love your partner every day."

BARBARA DE ANGELIS

"One advantage of marriage is that, when you fall out of love with him or he falls out of love with you, it keeps you together until you fall in again."

JUDITH VIORST

34 Love is reignited when...

You both agree up front about how you will raise your kids, parent as a unified front, and work out disagreements or misunderstandings in private.

35 Love is reignited when...

You spend a lot ... of time, not money.

36 Love is reignited when...

You take inventory of the attributes and virtues that each of you could hone to strengthen your love, then focus on cultivating those character strengths. (Flip to the appendix for a list of attributes. Which do each of you possess? Which should each of you cultivate? Circle the ones that you each want to work on and would like the other to consider, and view it as a fun project together).

37 Love is reignited when...

You each honor your word. (Under-promise and over-deliver. Empty promises are never forgotten. Say what you do and do what you say!)

38 Love is reignited when...

You can admit when you are wrong.

39 Love is reignited when...

Routine sex is anything but. (There is comfort in the way you have established your pattern, and in that comfort is a bond that provides a deep connection. It can be fulfilling and reassuring for both partners.)

40 Love is reignited when...

You realize that simple daily sacrifices (like opening her door, getting up to give him a welcome kiss, refilling her cup of coffee, investing some time in his hobby or just saying "thank you" for the tasks your partner performs routinely) can yield rewards far greater than any tangible gift.

41 Love is reignited when...

You make the effort to treat each other as though it were the first few months of your relationship – even when you've been together for ages.

42 Love is reignited when...

You handle all of life's curveballs as a team, making the decisions together. (This takes a bit of effort, since it might be hard to see eye to eye at first, but being able to come through the crisis hand in hand speaks volumes about your union.)

43 Love is reignited when...

You get excited about planning a trip together – even a short one – and put some real thought and effort into the best way for you to unwind and spend some time together. (This sends a message to your loved one that no matter how hectic things get, you take care of each other and want things to be special.)

44 Love is reignited when...

You make each other your top priority. (Work, kids, schedules, school, family obligations – everything else comes next. Knowing that there is at least one person out there who's looking out for you above everyone else will help you both get through some of life's toughest challenges.)

AGELESS RELATIONSHIP WISDOM

"Sex is emotion in motion."

MAE WEST

"Sex and beauty are inseparable, like life and consciousness.
And the intelligence which goes with sex and beauty,
and arises out of sex and beauty, is intuition."

DAVID HERBERT LAWRENCE

45 Love is reignited when...

You work together as a team to better navigate life's opportunities and challenges, following the guidelines:

TOGETHERNESS — Working together rather than as an individual, knowing you can make things happen more easily when you combine your efforts.

EMPATHY — Relating to each other, feeling concern for one another's well-being, and understanding each others core self.

ASSISTANCE — Desiring and being able to help whenever your partner needs some backup.

MATURITY — Being mature and fair; handling problems and challenges in a positive, constructive manner.

WORK — Getting the job done at home and in the workplace – meeting commitments, finishing the errands, delivering the service and winning the game.

ORGANIZATION — Organizing your day based on a mutual understanding of the roles each partner will play in family situations.

RESPECT — Appreciating the strengths and diversity that your partner brings to the table on a daily basis.

KINDNESS — Having compassion for and empowering your partner and those with whom you come into contact. (Generous deeds done for others speak volumes of love to your mate.)

46 Love is **reignited** when...

You remember that there are three ways to solve any problem:

WIN   WIN

WIN   LOSE

LOSE   LOSE

AGELESS RELATIONSHIP WISDOM

"It is not sex that gives the pleasure, but the lover."

MARGE PIERCY

"Sexual love is the most stupendous fact of the universe, and the most magical mystery our poor blind senses know."

AMY LOWELL

USE THIS SPACE TO WRITE ABOUT HOW YOU CAN
REIGNITE THE LOVE IN YOUR RELATIONSHIP

USE THIS SPACE TO WRITE ABOUT HOW YOU CAN
REIGNITE THE LOVE IN YOUR RELATIONSHIP

_____

_____

_____

_____

_____

_____

_____

_____

_____

_____

_____

_____

_____

_____

_____

_____

_____

_____

_____

_____

_____

Do you have unique ways to reignite love that you would like to share for future editions?
Please e-mail them for consideration to **loveisreignited@loveislost.com**.
(See submission terms at the back of this book.)

"Love is the compassion that cares,
the care that gets involved,
the commitment that sticks with a people through thick and thin!
Love is risk-taking when the flesh says look out for number one first.
Love is silence – when the words would hurt.
It is patience – when your neighbor's curt.
It is deafness – when scandal flows.
It is thoughtfulness – for others' woes.
It is promptness – when stern duty calls.
It is courage – when misfortune falls.
Love ever gives, forgives and outlives,
Ever stands with open hands.
And while it lives, it gives, for this is love's prerogative –
To give, and give, and give!"

JOHN PIPER

BIBLIOGRAPHY

American Heritage Talking Dictionary. The Learning Company, 1997.

Paget, Lou. *365 Days of Sensational Sex: Tantalizing Tips and Techniques to Keep the Fires Burning All Year Long.* Houder and Stroughton, 2004.

Phillips, Bob. *Book of Great Thoughts and Funny Sayings.* Tyndale House Publishers, 1993.

The Way: The Living Bible. Tyndale House Publishers, 1972.

COVER GRAPHIC PROVIDED BY LEFTRIGHT COLLABORATIVE
LeftRightCollaborative.com

APPENDIX

What are the attributes you need to hone? Which do you admire and appreciate in your spouse? Which ones do you wish he or she would work on? Go through this list together, and use different colored markers to circle the ones that need some attention AND, more importantly, the ones you appreciate in your partner.

Accepting	Composed	Efficient
Active	Conceptual	Empathetic
Adaptable	Conscientious	Enchanting
Adventuresome	Consistent	Energetic
Aesthetic	Constructive	Enlightening
Affectionate	Controlled	Entertaining
Alive	Convincing	Enthusiastic
Ambitious	Cool	Ethical
Analytic	Cooperative	Evolving
Appreciative	Courageous	Exciting
Articulate	Creative	Expressive
Astute	Curious	Facile
Attentive	Daring	Fair
Attractive	Decisive	Faithful
Authoritative	Dedicated	Fanciful
Autonomous	Deep	Fearless
Big-hearted	Dependable	Fiery
Bright	Detailed	Flamboyant
Businesslike	Determined	Flexible
Calm	Devoted	Fluent
Careful	Dignified	Forceful
Caring	Diligent	Forthright
Centered	Diplomatic	Fun-loving
Challenge-oriented	Direct	Generous
Charming	Dominant	Giving
Cheerful	Dramatic	Goal-oriented
Childlike	Driving	Good-natured
Clever	Durable	Graceful
Colorful	Dynamic	Grounded
Committed	Earthy	Gutsy
Compassionate	Effective	Hard-working

Helpful	Outgoing	Shrewd
Heroic	Outspoken	Sincere
Honest	Patient	Skillful
Honorable	Perfectionist	Socially Adept
Humorous	Persevering	Socially Responsible
Idealistic	Persuasive	Solid
Imaginative	Philosophical	Sophisticated
Incisive	Physical	Soulful
Independent	Pioneering	Spirited
Indomitable	Playful	Spiritual
Influential	Poised	Spontaneous
Innovative	Polished	Stable
Insightful	Positive	Steadfast
Inspirational	Powerful	Stimulating
Intellectual	Pragmatic	Strong-willed
Intense	Precise	Structured
Interesting	Productive	Successful
Intimate	Professional	Sunny
Intuitive	Progressive	Supportive
Inventive	Protective	Tasteful
Investigative	Prudent	Technical
Involved	Quick	Tenacious
Just	Realistic	Thorough
Knowledgeable	Reasonable	Tireless
Lively	Receptive	Tough
Logical	Resilient	Trustworthy
Loving	Resolute	Unassuming
Loyal	Resourceful	Undaunted
Lucid	Responsible	Unpretentious
Magnetic	Romantic	Unselfish
Memorable	Rousing	Up-to-date
Money-wise	Sagacious	Versatile
Moral	Seasoned	Vibrant
Motivated	Secure	Vigorous
Natural	Self-aware	Visionary
Noble	Self-confident	Vivacious
Nurturing	Self-expressive	Warm-hearted
Observant	Self-reliant	Well-grounded
Open	Self-sufficient	Well-liked
Optimistic	Sensitive	Witty
Orderly	Sensuous	Worldly
Organized	Service-oriented	Youthful

ABOUT THE AUTHORS

In their first book as co-authors, Sarah and Enrique Ruiz share the lessons and observations that brought them each through the ashes of lost love and helped them find each other and build a lasting love.

Sarah Ruiz was born in Boston, Massachusetts, and raised in New York City with a single mother and an older brother, wanting nothing more than to have the "whole-family" experience she missed out on growing up. After attending the University of Connecticut, she married young and had two beautiful girls. Through her own personal struggles and tragedies (including a divorce), her devotion to her daughters remained her first priority. She enrolled in business school, and years later, with her Masters in Business Administration (MBA) in hand, a new career opportunity brought her to Maryland, where she met and fell in love with Enrique.

Enrique Ruiz is a leading authority on Diversity & Inclusion methodology and practice. His 30-year career in Operations, managing teams of up to 15,000 people, and experience living on two continents gave him a reliable and effective perspective on people management that he now shares through his speeches and books on leadership, diversity, character building and relationships (visit *americas diversityleader.com*). He has a B.S. in Business from Excelsior College, University of New York, and recently completed the program for his MBA at the Heriot-Watt University in Edinburgh, Scotland.

After Enrique's failed 25-year marriage and the loss of his 18-year-old daughter, he began to transform his struggles into personal successes. He met Sarah while working on a government contract, and today they have found inner peace and a divine love.

Together, they have united a family of seven that is built on love, understanding, clarity and wisdom. Even with the normal ebb and flow of life, Enrique and Sarah began anew on their own journey to happily ever after. They hope their hard-earned wisdom will help you on yours. May your candle burn bright, all days, for life!

SUGGESTION SUBMISSIONS TERMS

Help other couples in their quest to recover, or discover, the relationships they want. Send suggestions or life experiences, along with your name, to the appropriate e-mail address (see below) for possible inclusion in future editions. You will receive an e-mail notification if your suggestion will be included, along with our edited version (if applicable) for your final review. While contributors will not receive any remuneration for submissions, we will give credit in the bibliography.

PLEASE SEND:

Suggestions for the *"Love Is Weakened When ..."* section to **loveisweakened@loveislost.com.**

Suggestions for the *"Love Is Felt When ..."* section to **loveisfelt@loveislost.com.**

Suggestions for the *"Love Is Reignited When ..."* section to **loveisreignited@loveislost.com.**

thank you!

LOST LOVE: THE GAME[©]

The Ultimate Relationship-Building Game for Couples

Get the board game where YOU already have all the answers! Build up enough Cupid bucks to "buy" your wedding rings and win the game by coming up with the most creative (and most win-win) solutions to common relationship issues. Play this fun and entertaining game of logic, emotion and courage with your partner, other couples, family members and friends. As you navigate the board and earn your bucks, you will learn more about your partner and get insight from the group on how to keep everyone's relationships strong!

ISBN 978-0-9827636-2-9

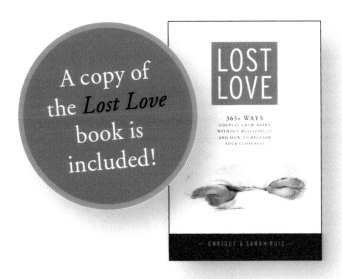

Order your personal toolset at
www.loveislost.com/game

D DETERMINATION

INDIVIDUALITY **I**

V VALUE

ENCOURAGEMENT **E**

R RESPECT

SYNERGY **S**

I INCLUSION

TALENT **T**

Y YOU

Book **Enrique Ruiz** to Speak at Your Next School, Conference or Corporate Event

Those who can see through the visible can achieve the impossible!

Looking for the perfect keynote speaker or presenter for your next conference, workshop, leadership training program or other corporate event? Let Enrique Ruiz empower and inspire your audience with his trademark presentations:

Tapping into the Silent Murmurs of Your Organization

Diversity appreciation is powerful. Numerous studies have shown that when companies and leaders really focus on it (not just pay it lip-service), diversity can make a huge impact on not only morale, but also on the bottom line! So, how do you truly diversify – beyond quotas and policies – and effectively build an inclusive workforce? You uncover the diamonds within your organization by tapping into the quiet murmur of thoughts in each and every employee.

The Power of Transformation: Diversity and Me

Each individual has a unique history – one that includes experiences, culture, faith, family, survival and education – and so each of us has a completely unique vantage point. These differing perspectives, if properly and fully tapped, can offer a tremendous competitive advantage to organizations. By understanding how people from different backgrounds tick, and fostering a culture where everyone feels respected, accepted and appreciated, you can create a stronger, more productive and engaged workforce – which will boost morale, innovation *and* revenue!

A History of Discrimination, and How to Change Your Own Discriminating Behavior

Because we cannot fully understand the present and effectively mold the future without understanding our pasts and ourselves, Enrique examines the history of discrimination and answers all the questions about other races and religions most of us are afraid to ask for fear of seeming racist or ignorant. Even more importantly, audience members will begin to recognize their own hidden biases and prejudices – and begin to better understand and appreciate, as well as communicate and collaborate with, individuals from different backgrounds – so they can build bridges of trust that propel their companies forward in our increasingly competitive (and increasingly global) economy.

Wisher to Washer: How to Move from Just Existing to Personal Abundance

Imagine the future that you want. Is it different from where you are now? Do you think you have what it takes to be successful? Are you a leader with vision, values, mission and purpose? Are you equipped with the ingredients necessary to create the life you want to live? There are three types of people – *Wishers, Washers* and *Wishy-Washys.* Most wish, some flounder and few excel. Find out how you can move from just existing, to personal abundance!

TO BOOK ENRIQUE FOR YOUR NEXT EVENT, CALL 540.446.3164 OR E-MAIL
enrique@americasdiversityleader.com

Wisher, Washer, Wishy-Washy:
How to Move From Just Existing to Personal Abundance

Imagine the future that you want. Is it different from where you are now? Do you think you have what it takes to be successful? Are you a leader with vision, values, mission and purpose? Are you equipped with the ingredients necessary to create the life you want to live? Why does only 5 percent of the population attain phenomenal success while many others lead lives of quiet desperation? Is it luck? Genes? Age? Environment? Nope. Most people dream of success but, as they grow older, settle into believing that life got in the way, that their unfulfilled dreams and unachieved goals were simply not meant to be. Not true. It is a matter of choice and of persistence, coupled with dogged determination in the face of obstacles, setbacks and failures. Success, when you've scaled the mountain and really earned it, is so much sweeter. And wishing for success and committing yourself to it are two very different things. So, are you a *Wisher* or a *Washer,* or just plain *Wishy-Washy?*

www.wisherwasher.com

The "W" Characters: How to Get What You Want AND Make a Difference in the World

Children understand far more than most adults give them credit for. As a society, we teach children how to do things and the difference between right and wrong. We answer their questions (as much as possible) about what and why things are. But children are also capable of understanding much deeper life principles – like the importance of building character, how to make decisions, the consequences of relying on others to make their dreams come true and the value of their word. In this story of a group of children who gather for an overnight camping trip that changes their young lives, *The "W" Characters* gets these messages across in a fun, easy-to-read presentation that they'll want to read again and again.

www.characterforchildren.com

Discriminate or Diversify: Those Who Can See
Through the Visible Can Achieve the Impossible!

Knowledge is power, and so is Diversity! Understanding and appreciating the unique differences that each race, sex, ethnicity, personality, age group, religion and other subcultures bring to the table will not only make you a more enlightened person and a more effective leader, but it can also boost your organization's bottom line (and *your* career) in a big way. In *Discriminate or Diversify*, Ruiz explores our history of discrimination, provides informed profiles on the many groups of people that make our world so interesting and exciting, and offers solutions for how to build a culture of Diversity and Inclusion in your organization. When you can see through the *visible*, you can achieve the impossible!

www.humandiversity.biz

Made in the USA
Charleston, SC
15 April 2013